Brown Gal in the Rain

Brown Gal in the Rain

By

Indrani Chowdhury

I dedicate this book to my mother Mrs. Kakali Chowdhury, the first teacher of my life. She is a born fighter and an amazing woman, whom I have always admired.

I love you Ma!

From the Author's Desk

By now, I believe I have a rough understanding of how the real-world works. But I must admit that I am not a big fan of it as its daily mechanisms tend to tire you down. In contrast to most 'professionals' that I see in and around me, my sensibilities always nudge me to meander in the less-trodden alleys to discover that succulence of life, the procurement of which transforms this otherwise dreary existence into an outstanding experience. I believe that it cannot be understood through conventional systems of understanding, as this elixir remains hidden in the chaos that exists within all of us. You have to know how to extract it from there. Everything starts from within. So, the game is that you must take a plunge of faith and dive in there, explore the labyrinths of your own darkness (it's alright if you are afraid initially), hear the voices that are screaming to have an audience with you, and finally smuggle some pearls from your very own underworld. These pearls may be your innermost dreams, fantasies, absurd, and abstract ideas, your confrontation with different worlds and extraction of buried truths from there, the knowledge of which finally shapes your true being. Now they become the raw materials of your unique creation, waiting to be explored by you. I have smuggled my pearls (read poems) from the deep recesses of my inner realm. Each one of them is special to me as they have enriched my sensibilities while taking their shape through my ideas, words, rhythm, and style. So, what are you waiting for? Read them to see the world through my eyes!

Indrani Chowdhury

Acknowledgements

I would like to thank my family members who provided constant support and encouragement to me while writing this book.

Secondly, I would like to thank Manoj Krishnan sir, founder of the Asian Literary Society, without whose guidance and support this book would not have seen the light of day.

Finally, I would like to thank the Asian Literary Society and Notion Press for taking my book under their wing.

Indrani Chowdhury is a visionary poet/author from India who creates evocative literary pieces that transcend boundaries. Her writings invite readers on a profound journey, exploring themes of love, identity, and the complexities of existence. In 2021, her book 'Raining Drops of Rainbow Verses' was published, which won numerous accolades from her readers. According to her, as words come pouring into her mind, she sits and joins them into meaningful wholes and presents them to her readers. She claims it to be an extraordinary experience to be able to represent her ideas through her words. It has now become her tool to make soulful connections with other like-minded individuals, to give voice to relevant causes, and to enrich her existence by embarking on an interesting journey towards purposeful living. She has been the recipient of many awards and has co-authored almost thirty anthologies to date.

Foreword

Indrani Chowdhury is an erudite poet from India who has won many accolades in the Asian Literary Society. Many international literary luminaries have applauded her amazing skills to weave a tapestry of emotions. Indrani has mastered the skill of writing on diverse topics ranging from deep emotions to social issues. She has been the recipient of many awards and has contributed to many anthologies to date.

Through her writings, Indrani raises many thought-provoking questions that keep resonating in the reader's mind. She has always shared her point of view beautifully and it often enthralls the wider audience. Her writings invite readers on a profound journey, exploring different hues of life.

In the book 'Brown Gal in the Rain', the first thing that attracted me was the different sections of poems under headings such as Ballads of Heart, Hues of Life, Peekaboo, Let There Be Light, Grazing the Meadows of Nature, and Lightweight Singles. I liked this concept and loved the poems in each of them.

Though all poems in this book are quite good, I would like to mention the name of one poem titled 'One Final Look, One Final Touch'. I have read the poem multiple times. Its last few lines are simple yet hold deep emotions and that is the beauty of Indrani's writing.

Now She knew.

She was hungry for one final look, one final touch,
In the unfinished book of her mortal life,
Before crossing over to the other side.

I would also like to quote her poem 'Eyes'. In these few lines, she covered the reality of life that we often ignore.

If eyes are a window to one's soul,
Then how do illusions play at what we behold?
The thing is, our eyes see what it wants to see,
Turning a blind eye to the harsh reality.

Like these, there are many other poems that will keep the readers hooked into the book.

In 2021, her book 'Raining Drops of Rainbow Verses' was published, which won numerous accolades from her readers and was a worthy read. I hope her new book will also get a similar response.

I admire her dedication and immense passion for poetry. As ALS community founder, I am glad to see her growth which is inspiring many authors.

I extend my heartiest congratulations and best wishes to Indrani Chowdhury for her latest book.

Regards
Manoj Krishnan
Founder, Asian Literary Society

Index

From the Author's Desk

Acknowledgements

Foreword

A.   Ballads of Heart

1.   Brown Gal in the Rain   18

2.   A Night Kissed Tale of Love

        and Longing   20

3.   Love is in the Air!   22

4.   The Werewolf and the Princess
        (Narrative Poem)   25

5.   The Wasteland Called My Heart   36

6.   I Wish a Writer Had Loved Me...   38

7.   My Beautiful Dreams About You   40

8.   I Had Always Waited for This

        Rain...   44

9.   Until We Meet Again(Loop Poetry) 46

10.   My Beloved Niece   48

11.   Dearest Indradip (Epistolary Poem) 50

12.   You are Mine and I am Yours   52

13.   My Heart Goes On (Epistolary Poem) 55

14.	One Final Look, One Final Touch	60
15.	But Then, What Do They Know?	64
16.	I Wonder, Was it My Heart?	
	(Abstract Poem)	66
17.	Old School	68
18.	Ruined	70
19.	My Valentine Tale	72
20.	My Telephonic Romance	74
21.	The Mermaids' Ramp	76
B.	**Hues of Life**	
1.	O Life, Colour Me with Your Hues	80
2.	The Song of Life	83
3.	The City	85
4.	The Song of Life	87
5.	Dear Life...	90
6.	Paper Boats	92
7.	Let My Lies Prevail	94
8.	Rewinding Life.	96
9.	So, Can You Hear Me?	98
10.	Stateless	100
11.	Time's Gift	102

12.	Time's Tentacles	104
13.	Nostalgia	106
14.	The Books That Had Shaped My Life	108
15.	Mahatma	110
16.	My Poems Matters	112
17.	Camera Moments	114
18.	Memories of Happiness	116
19.	Mother-An Eternal Soul	118
20.	Maa	120
21.	How to Make a Perfect Christmas Dough (List Poetry)	123
C.	**Peekaboo!**	
1.	The Child Within Me	126
2.	I Am Still a Child at Heart	128
D.	**Let There Be Light!**	
1.	The Dreams of My Heart (Janaku)	131
2.	The She Saga	134
3.	My Dear Girl, You Must Know...	136
4.	Unfulfilled Dream	138
5.	My Life's Learning	140

6.	Letters of Parvati	142
7.	Wonder Woman's Appraisal of the Superwomen of this World	145
8.	Tale of a Transwoman	148
9.	Diary of a 'Different' Girl	149
10.	Dear Facebook girl...	152
11.	My Menstruation Story	154
12.	Greetings To All Women!	157
13.	Prometheus Unbound	159

E. Grazing the Meadows of Nature

1.	The Redeemer Night	162
2.	Ode to Spring	165
3.	Summer's Last Lament	167
4.	It's October again!	168
5.	The Frosty Friend	170
6.	How Much was Too Much? (Pentastich poem)	172
7.	Lavender Smile	174
8.	An Ode to the Sunflower	176
9.	Homecoming	178
10.	The Magnanimous Mountain	180
11.	Ode to a Sparrow	182

| 12. | Fireflies | 184 |
| 13. | The Travelogue of a Hyacinth Girl | 186 |

F.   **Lightweight Singles**

1.	Pain	189
2.	Memories	190
3.	What You Want to be?	191
4.	Marriage	192
5.	Graveyard	193
6.	Bangles	194
7.	Souq	195
8.	Arrows	196
9.	Let Me Be....	197
10.	Strings	198
11.	Fire	199
12.	Eyes	200

A.

Ballads of Heart

1. Brown Gal in the Rain

This time, the rain has drenched my soul,

As I have walked down the miles with you –

With a throbbing heart and a toddler's smile,

Rejoicing the moment of my eternal love.

This time, the rain has presented an uncluttered view,

Of your ignited thoughts and piercing eyes –

That searches my presence, my affirmation,

In calm and chaos, in reality, and illusions.

This time, the rain has joined my part, that is, you,

With my whole being, like conjoined twins –

As we dance like peacocks, playfully putting the leaves above our heads,

Building a luminous constellation of united hearts.

This time, the soft pitter-patter of the rain on the leaves echoed those sentiments,

Which, without this rain, would have remained unspoken, unaddressed, unresolved –

I wish I could tell you how like the rain you are,

A savior, a magic potion of nourishment, rescuing me from my mundane existence.

2. A Night Kissed Tale of Love and Longing

The nocturnal universe witnessed their cherishing dream,

As they immersed themselves in building their love nest,

By erecting a cozy tent amidst this kingdom of wilderness,

And by making a bonfire, near their nestled crèche.

The trees in their vicinity created a dark, impenetrable wall,

As if protecting their Garden of Eden from the outside, vicious world.

And the love birds resembled glow-worms, glowing in the fire,

As if waiting to be burned down in their own desires.

As the fallen leaves rustled musically with the soft breeze,

They huddled together to press their lips.

The star-studded, revealing sky again reiterated a cosmic tale.

And they spotted with wonder a shooting star.

"Make a wish! Make a wish!", he murmured to her.

She pondered a bit, and then announced softly,

"I have you by my side, what more can I wish, my dear?"

3. Love is in the Air!

A soft silvery luminescence cradled the night,

And the lovers nestled in its arms.

The enigmatic night now started playing,

Hide and seek with the cascading silvering beams,

Ushering an enchanting realm of love and
dreams.

Those two who defied the draconian rules of
their world,

Stood there dropping down their guard,

Revealing their true selves,

To revel in the carnival of love.

First, their eyes met, then their hands touched,
and then their lips locked,

Conquering the length and breadth of one
another in love.

A spirit of exhilaration now heightened their
sensation,

And they attempted to break free from all
shackles and inhibitions.

Their silhouettes mixed and matched as if they were attuned with,

The lambent-umbra phase orchestrated by this nocturnal hippodrome.

An aura of refulgence surfaced there,

As the two waltzed side by side,

To further enhance the performance of the thaumaturge night.

The heathen night then schemed to cover their tracks,

As they dived deep in love to be wrecked, to be saved.

The jubilation then followed by a jamboree,

As the silky moonlight caressed their bodies,

Like a lover intended to shower perennial bliss.

Then the hasnahanas bloomed in manifold hues,

Crafting a floral gazebo for the two.

As the two rolled there,

Smilingly gazing at the woolgatherer moon above,

A quiet chaos built up in them leading to an epiphany.

They realized then that they must strive to remain together,

To sing and live this amaranthine ballad of their journey.

4. The Werewolf and the Princess (Narrative Poem)

Prologue

That night,

The moon at first cradled a soft luminescence,

Half revealing, half concealing the clandestine affairs of its dark realm,

Almost monopolizing its right to narrate,

About how it all began.

This cabalistic tale could be dismissed,

Applying the narrow perimeters of mortal reason.

But the moon had witnessed enough seasons,

To know that some things do happen beyond reason.

Canto-1

Reddrik, the Werewolf

That night,

As the moon designed a unique stage,

Where light and shadow played hide and seek,

The manifold shades of truth and falsehood,

The werewolf firmly stood,

Facing the intimidating royal castle of Armetedia,
beyond the woods.

The other wolves while patrolling the dark alleys
of their wood,

Uneasily howled, sensing the werewolf's
supernatural presence.

They could feel it in their guts that he was
invincible,

And they shouldn't interfere with his business.

That night,

He then howled, rupturing the pervading silence,

Sending a chill down the spines of the living.

Its deafening sound echoed throughout,

Affirming the presence of his supernatural being.

But though his eyes generated a hellish fire,
revealing his ferocity,

It, however, somehow also gave away his
vulnerability.

He reasoned that though in this life of his everything seemed new,

Everything was the same.

For tonight, like all those other nights of his past lives,

He would lay his claim.

That night,

While he stood there, burning in his own desire,

His mind traveled several light years.

He reminisced how he first met her,

While participating in a hunting game, in their kingdom of Reddender.

In that birth, he was a prince called Reddrik by name,

And she was a princess Nina from the kingdom of Dames.

Amid the game as their eyes locked, it changed everything.

For they both could feel a unique tie of belonging.

They were in love, they were in love,

And it echoed in their ground beneath and in the heavens above.

Ah! His heart ached,

As he remembered those promises made to each other,

But that could not be kept.

Right after their betrothal,

He suffered a premature death.

It so happened that while defending the honor of his country on the battlefield,

He succumbed to his injuries after fighting with great zeal.

Many a time in his emotional outbursts,

He had declared that their love was cursed.

And he believed it till now.

As fate had designed such a complicated stratagem,

That hitherto, they could not fulfill their vow.

Every time in his pursuit to achieve her, through fair or unfair means,

He was defeated, beaten, caged, or killed by forces stronger than him.

But though he had kept her waiting so long, pining for him,

In her every consecutive life,

They remained united in her dreams.

For in her every life, she could feel her presence,

In her heart, in her essence.

It was destiny that she would accept him in all shapes, sizes, and form.

It was destiny that she would come to him, defying societal norms.

Canto-2

Amelia (Nina) the Princess

That night,

As the silver moon created an illusionary state with its silver beams,

Half revealing, half concealing the werewolf's nocturnal schemes,

Amelia, the beloved princess of Armenia,

Felt again the palpable presence of him,

In the deep recesses of her recurring dream.

It seemed that she with all her worldly power and possessions,

Couldn't bar his intrusion in her subconscious domain.

And was it not true that now-a-days,

She almost looked forward to his invasions in her inner realm?

So, though betrothed to the formidable king of Seven States,

This time, she did not hesitate from letting him crush her chaste lips in her dreams.

But little did she know that this kiss of his would change everything,

As it would unlock her memory, making her remember the past happenings.

That night,

She suddenly awoke past midnight.

Widely awake now, she sat in her bed upright,

Dreading the reemergence of her inner tirades of emotions,

In those wee hours of the night.

But much to her surprise, a strange calmness engulfed her,

As if she had solved an intricate puzzle that had so long baffled her.

She experienced an epiphany,

Tantamount to an inner reawakening journey,

As her mind was flooded with memories of those happenings,

Which undeniably pointed to the fact that in all her past mortal lives,

She had loved only him.

That night,

The moon now glowed with an iridescent golden sheen,

And the dulcet tone of the soft wind soothsaid that a new story would begin.

As Amelia stood before her chamber's casement ajar,

Her eyes wandered beyond the palace boundary, darting afar.

There, in the uncharted territory of the woods, she saw him.

What gave him away this time was his eyes, which summarized their connection.

She now knew that he who stood there, pining for her, was her only destination.

She could not run away from him,

Nor did she aspire for it, as her heart rose to mutiny,

This time she made a strong resolution to unite with him by fighting her adverse destiny.

Her hasty footfalls remained imprinted with the sonorous music of the night,

As she embarked on her journey to become the werewolf's bride.

Canto-3

Patrick, the Archer

That night,

As the moon metamorphosed to a red blood orb,

And the blood moon oozed blood in the milieu of that part of the globe,

The temperature soared capturing the shift of tone in the environs' temperament,

It was as if nature buckled up to act as a prop in this saga's next segment.

For the actions of Patrick, the royal archer was about to begin,

Which would be instrumental in changing the trajectory of this story with a whole new spin.

Long before the princess, Patrick had located 'it',

From the eye hole of the palace door.

He shuddered to find the presence of such a demonic creature,

Right from the pages of legends and folklore.

While his mind raced to comprehend the incomprehensible,

His intuition signalled that he now had to rumble with this trouble.

Lo! Who was there? Was it not the princess?

Where was she going on such a night with haste?

And why? Had she been enamoured by this ominous creature?

So, it seemed to him that she was enchanted with it,

And in her trance state walking towards it,
oblivious of the danger!

This is not a time of deliberation or indecision,

For the princess must be rescued with action
done with precision.

So, he concentrated and aimed,

His silver arrow with firm determination to upset
the werewolf's nefarious game.

And as he finally released it with full might,

In that sinister setting, a giant owl cried.

Epilogue

That night,

As the moon finally settled in the midst of foggy,
obfuscating clouds,

The events of the night got more shrouded in
mystery beyond doubt.

The werewolf, however, had seen both the
princess and the arrow racing towards him,

But he resolved to stand there, curious to know
what this time fate had stored for him.

Would fate again defeat him with its wicked
schemes?

Or would their love outlast their painful past and
a new dawn would begin?

That night,

The moon sighed and waited with bated breath
along with the wolf,

For fate had assigned it the role of an immaculate
record tool.

And as the werewolf stood there without
inhibitions,

And with an open heart, bursting with pride,

What do you think would touch him first?

The lethal arrow or his amorous bride?

5. The Wasteland Called My Heart

In my heart, the dirge reached its crescendo,

And a death knell sounded for the hitherto
growing sapling of love in it,

As you left for your heavenly abode ditching life,

Transcending forever the temporal and timeless
lines.

I knew not what now left of me,

A stupendous, almost deafening silence had
engulfed my heart.

And as the realization dawned on me that,

All my tears and silent prayers would yield no
result,

It crushed the green, love-laced meadows of my
heart,

Rapidly transforming it into a desolated,
abandoned graveyard.

And as you embarked upon a journey unknown,
all alone,

After the granules of sands of time had slipped
from your hand,

I too was banished to suffer forever,

In the vicious quagmire of my remaining life's
loveless wasteland.

6. I Wish a Writer Had Loved Me...

I wish a writer loved me, as he could replicate with his ink-

The roaring delights of the savage lightning,

Or the exact aroma of my mother's ambrosial cooking.

The carefree beauty of a nameless, vagabond flower, bloomed in the wilderness,

Or the cotton candy clouds moving with its usual, youthful zest.

The irresistible urge to lock lips with my soul mate,

Or the flamingo's waltz to please its chosen date.

The gentle rustle of an unhurried, languid wind,

Or the brittle sound in a rain- soaked roof of tin.

The virile waves seducing the stationary rocks,

Or the azure sky broadcasting its beautiful blue cloak.

The masked arrogance of a rapidly cascading waterfall,

Or the kindred spirit of an accommodating, shadowy tree tall.

The bursting happiness of a heart fraught with hope,

Or the storm's rage bringing the faint- hearts catastrophe.

These ongoing songs of senses breathe the fire of life in me,

As such I sincerely wish a writer loved me.

7. My Beautiful Dreams About You

Hidden from the grim realities of my real life,

There is a safely guarded place in my heart where
all my dreams reside.

It is in these dreams where you exist,

With all the colors, with all the twists.

'Ordinary' is the word that defines me,

A genuine awkward fellow who they call
'wooden'.

I don't mind though their name-calling me,

As I do not remain so with you in our
conversations.

We talk together, laugh together,

Which is a good thing,

You know it is a privilege for me,

To share with you my life's little things.

You know me,

From the bottom of your heart,

Never minding my stuttering and clumsiness,

Never minding my faded color shirts.

I consider myself a repeat offender,

In upsetting our romantic conversations,

By often talking then about my failures,

A topic, which seems to have become my
obsession.

But that's what love is all about,

Where you can lay bare your soul,

Without becoming an object of pity,

For the other side as a whole.

I thank my stars for winning your love,

It surely is a big thing for me.

As only in your gracious presence,

I feel alive, I truly break free.

You have touched those chords of my heart,

Which I thought never existed.

Now I think kindly about myself,

The thing that I have so long foolishly resisted.

For a long time, I have searched for an emphatic soul,

Who could truly understand me,

A kindred soul who would extend her hand,

Rescuing me from the vicious loop of self-pity.

My love, you have truly rescued me from that loop,

And lifted me from it quite high.

Now I can have an uncluttered view of everything,

With you there by my side.

My dream of being with you,

Let me keep going in real.

Since you have bound me with the thread of love,

In my dreams, I feel healed.

The best part is that you are patient with me,

Giving me space to bloom in my own time and terms.

This is truly a precious thing to me,

As it has been denied to me in the real world.

I sincerely pray to my maker that,

Let these dreams of mine always exist,

For it is here that I can see all the colors of the world,

And experience life's amazing twists.

8. I Had Always Waited for This Rain...

The lost rhythms of my heart had found its tune again,

I knew that you were there for me, as I knew that it had rained.

I thought I could forget you-

But, in the green meadows of my mind,

You always existed, like rain, which when showers,

Makes the long dry months a lost memory-

Makes it feel like a long, forgotten pain.

You did downpour heavily,

Wetting the deepest recesses of my unconscious self,

And I bloomed like a rare desert flower-

Embracing my metamorphosis, my true self.

It rained, rained, and rained,

Until it washed away all my inhibitions-

And before I knew it, you were painting the canvas of my heart,

With the color red, raining your love lessons.

You challenged my beliefs that I could exist,

Would exist, without your presence by my side-

But now I knew the truth, and would not fight it again,

Now I knew that I had always waited for your revival, I had always waited for this rain.

The lost rhythms of my heart had found its tune again,

I knew that you were there for me, as I knew that it had rained.

9. Until We Meet Again...(Loop Poetry).

Adieu! my love, until we meet again,

Again, when the vernal cloak will be adorned by nature,

Nature, which is known for its unparalleled beauty,

Beauty, which is sprinkled in birds, beasts, and flowers,

Flowers, which cover the rustic paths with colors,

Colors, which rejuvenate the life of the mortals,

Mortals, who dream of a rainbow-coloured life,

Life, which is known for its manifold struggles,

Struggles, which strengthen our spirit and resolutions,

Resolutions, which bring our long -awaited achievements,

Achievements, which reward us a with a meaningful existence,

Existence, which remains incomplete without love,

Love, yes, love will only shine in our eyes,

Eyes, which will be longing for our union,

Union, which will be due for a long, until we meet again...adieu!

10. My Beloved Niece

A snowball, when first born,

A red cherry in the following months,

Born in February with a freshness,

Like a beautiful flower with a fragrance.

My niece stole my heart,

The very day we locked our eyes,

The story that ensued henceforth,

Is of perennial bliss and an unbreakable tie.

I am surprised by her sensibility,

That she understands me so well,

We are two musketeers, having each other's back,

The rest of the world can go to hell.

She has touched those long-forgotten, dusty
chords,

Which, long unused, had rusted in my heart,

She laughs and lo! She ignites in me,

An inexplicable, euphoric, rhythmic part.

Though small, her world is big,

Encompassing all fairies, birds, beasts, and
flowers,

A little girl, with a heart of gold, she has taught
me,

To live by moments and not by hours.

Note: This poem is dedicated to my beloved
niece Dhrity Chowdhury.

11. Dearest Indradip (Epistolary Poem)

Dearest Indradip,

Your presence in my life,

Seems to prophesize that I would change for the better,

As I am now your mother.

That cherubic smile of yours reflects your innocence,

Saves me from my decadence,

And serves as a panacea,

Curing all my insecurities, and vanities, ending all my grievances.

As I fall for you a little more every day,

And yearn to be your closest ally in every way,

I become humble thanking the almighty,

For rekindling my life by giving you to me,

A boon, which has unfailingly set me free.

You must know that you are my heart and soul,

My part and my whole,

The quintessential essence of my being.

You are that pristine beating heart,

Who is entwined in my everything.

I now dare to walk the untrodden path,

Do not fear to love others with all my heart,

Because I have you.

And something tells me that it would remain so,

As you would make sure that I adore,

This life of mine while having this joyous ride
with you.

Love Ma.

Note: This poem is dedicated to my beloved son
Indradip Basu.

12. You are Mine and I am Yours

He said to her,

"I wonder whether you remember the day,

When I stood with bated breath,

To utter those three words to be said to you."

She smiled while settling her white hairs with her hands and replied,

"What a thing to ask!

Of course, I do.

But for some other reasons, I tell you.

I remember it for your nervous smile,

The droplets of sweat on your forehead,

And those deep brown eyes of yours which entreated me,

To break the ice and help you to go ahead."

He protested and said,

"That's not true!

For what I felt then,

You felt it too!

Don't you agree with me that you always knew,

That I truly meant to say those three words that day to you?"

With a mock surprise in her eyes, she said,

"Well, well, well,

Was that your plan?

But as much as I can remember now,

You did what you can.

May I remind you,

That you skipped that part,

Where you had to say to me 'I Love You', clear and loud,

Instead, very softly muttered something,

What I am sure could not be heard!"

He looked at her now again with those deep brown eyes,

That did not let her that day to think twice,

Before saying those three words to him.

As now she could feel,

The rising rhythm of her throbbing heart,

She lowered her eyes and said finally,

"When both your language and courage failed,

To say to me what must be said,

I then said those very words to you,

By taking the plunge of faith.

For how could I not let you know,

That you are mine and I am yours."

13. My Heart Goes On (Epistolary Poem).

Dearest Deep,

Had I known that,

My brief rendezvous with your heart,

Would have had such a profound impact on me,

I would have consciously tried not to fall so
deeply in love with you,

I would have tried harder to refrain myself from
loving you.

Why do you ask? Oh, why?

Because you own me now my love!

I assure you own me completely now.

My happiness now lies,

In the sweet remembrance of your smile.

And it's tormenting for me,

If you are away from my side.

Before the 'fall',

I was alone but not lonely,

If not happy, live peacefully.

But I cannot say this now about myself.

This frequent surge of ebb and flow of my
emotional tides is,

Always taking me on a roller coaster ride.

Sometimes, as if I fall faint with happiness, with
joyous abandon,

But the very next moment,

I tire myself out fearing what might happen.

On the other hand,

I doubt whether I ever in my past had felt so free!

My love, I am at a total loss of words to describe
this new me.

The very fact that I have loved someone with
such honesty,

Ennoble me in my own eyes, I assure thee.

I can feel that I have become more emphatic,

More forgiving, more sympathetic in my dealings,

It is as if I now get a clearer picture of others'
feelings.

I can see through their words, their eyes,

Their very love, loss, and pain.

A phenomenal change has taken place,

In my emotional domain.

I am sure that you doubt now,

Whether you have loved someone,

Who is a bundle of contradictions?

You now doubt me as a girl,

Who cannot even handle her own emotions?

But I will not complain about it, my love.

Because you know, the truth is,

You are thinking about me in all this.

And it makes me feel good, gives me some peace.

I remember,

The plan was to never divulge,

These minute details of my heart to you.

The plan was to act exotic, hard to get,

Way out of your league Frau.

But soon I realized that,

My own heart was revolting against my own plan.

It persistently egged me on and on,

To take you as much as into confidence with
time.

And then, thank God,

You unabashedly divulged your feelings for me.

The rest is history.

But though I could not play with great panache,

The game of love like some other girls,

Though I could not play hard to get,

And act as if I am a priceless pearl,

But I am sure that by now you know that,

You have loved a true gem.

I am sure that by now you have realized that,

You have truly won the game.

For I could be a bundle of contradictions,

But what is more important is,

I am true to my emotions.

I live, love, cry, and laugh,

Never feel ashamed to reveal to you my simple heart.

I know for sure that it is this simplicity of mine,

That you value so much.

As it is a rare quality,

In this complex world of ours.

My love,

My heart goes on and on thinking about you.

It has now remained the only relevant fact of my life,

It has now remained my only truth.

Yours forever

Indrani.

14. One Final Look, One Final Touch.

She scrutinized the half-embroidered tablecloth,

The first thing she had looked for after her arrival here,

Her expert-practiced eyes,

Soon detecting the sharp needle, still attached at one of its edges.

One of the many of her half-done things,

Like her half-lived life,

Abruptly cut short by an unfortunate happening.

She sighed and then shuddered thinking,

Until yesterday,

Everything was colorful, perfectly radiant,

Until yesterday,

When the car crash happened.

She sat introspecting in her home's living room,

Freshly bedecked with fashionable Aztec printed cushions,

Her cushions, still carrying her sweet, faint smell,

Oblivious of the predicament, that had befallen.

A faint smile escaped from her lips,

As her eyes fondled the photograph,

Strategically stationed at their newly polished
mahogany center table.

She now reasoned that it seemed,

More like a perfect painting than a photograph,

Revealing a fully smitten Dipto's unmasked pride,

After winning her hand as his bride.

She again sensed the hunger arising in her,

For his caresses and kisses.

Soon she gave in, savoring her feelings for him,

Savoring her rising emotional tide.

He surely hadn't suspected that she was carrying,

Before leaving for his overseas project.

Or did he? She wondered.

Then, she reasoned that it was too early,

For a thick head like him to detect the signs,

The reasons for her radiant smiles and rampant
mood swings.

She had wanted to keep the things that way,

To narrate their baby's arrival,

Sound like a fairy tale,

To her man when he would return after two
weeks.

A sudden surge of pain arose from her stomach
and

It seemed to puncture her heart,

Before becoming the cause of the lump now
forming in her throat.

She wondered why she came here,

To relive the hurt, to relive the pain,

Rather than staying at the morgue,

With her battered mortal remains,

Before embarking on her journey on an
unknown road.

Now she knew.

She was hungry for one final look, one final
touch,

In the unfinished book of her mortal life,

Before crossing over to the other side.

15. But Then, What Do They Know?

They say we are not meant to be together,

Not meant to be called 'soul mates.'

But then, what do they know?

Do they know that,

We have always resided in each other's hearts.

That though we have fallen out publicly,

Yet have always pined for each other's touch?

Do they know that what we have said on record,

The blame games of varied sorts are,

In actuality desperate attempts on our part,

To make each other aware of one another's
faults, so that,

Next time, we both refrain,

From pressing each other's trigger points,

And could live amicably, ending this discord?

And finally, do they know that,

We both are trying in our foolish ways,

To hold on to the hope that,

All would be well between us again,

As in between us so much love for each other has still remained?

16. I Wonder, Was it My Heart?
(Abstract Poem)

The vagabond stood upon the crimson sea,

A rough night or a tough call?

It couldn't be determined, it seemed.

Lo! Now the sea halved to devour him with its humongous gulp.

Nevertheless, he stood and trampled on something.

I wonder, was it my heart?

I gasped even in my dream state,

As he greedily showcased his hatred.

Was he a lover boy or an oddball? A busybody or nobody?

It couldn't be determined, it seemed.

And now the sharks arrived to crush him with all their might!

Their sharp teeth reveled at the taste of his blood.

But he withstood the ravages done by them,

And remained busy trampling that thing.

I wonder, was it my heart?

Now I screamed in that bottomless dream.
But the droplets of blood from the crimson sea
overpowered me.
I screamed and screamed without a voice.
But the vagabond gazed at me with his bloodshot
eyes, hearing the 'noise'!
Was he a crusader or a brooder?
A ghost rider or a murderer?
Nothing could define him, it seemed.
He again busied himself trampling that thing.
I wonder, was it my heart?

17. Old School

My love,

I prefer to touch and feel,

Your love-filled, racing heart,

With my own hands,

Than to attend your long distant calls,

From faraway lands.

Dearest,

I prefer to read your letters,

Which may have errors in spelling,

And is a testimony,

Of your poor vocabulary,

Than reading your auto correct,

Spell checked, clean handwriting,

Electronic mails,

Which reads bizarrely formal,

And as such grossly inappropriate,

In matter of feelings.

My life,

I prefer those old joints,

Where amidst commotion,

We still remain drunken,

By tasting the magic potion,

Called love,

Than to meet in a proper restaurant,

With champagne on our table,

And a uniformed butler,

Hovering above.

That's because my love,

Your touch, your handwritten words,

Or your presence,

Reveals the real you.

Like a speech impromptu.

Forgive me, my love,

If I sound like an emotional fool,

For in matters of heart,

I am still old school.

18. Ruined

The moment you uttered, "We are done!"

The apocalypse began,

Causing chasms, life-threatening concussions,

And a black hole in my heart.

It felt as if a thunderous comet had,

Ripped apart my consciousness,

And for that matter, whatever mattered till then,

And an ominous, almost deafening silence, had
begun to set in,

In that post-apocalyptic realm.

This time, there was something,

In your tone and I knew that,

Your verdict could not be postponed.

It screamed that everything had ended-

And all my pleadings and prayers would now fall
on deaf ears,

This time, it could not be mended.

But what did hurt was,

That you never really had loved me,

And was playing with my feelings all along.

But wasn't it strange, how it felt so right to me for
so long,

When it was truly, so wrong?

19. My Valentine Tale

I loved that boy who made me my first paper
boat,

I loved that girl who helped to keep it afloat.

I loved that bell which ushered the school
vacation,

I loved that train which took me to a hill station.

I loved my cousins who took me under their
wings,

I loved my brother who gifted me those earrings.

I loved those days when my nonsense actions
were not frowned upon,

I loved that place which embraced me as its own.

I loved my parents who endured my adolescence
storm,

I loved that neighbor who baked a cake for our
home.

I loved that mirror which announced me as
beautiful,

I loved those books which made my reading
joyful.

I loved that man who shamelessly kissed me,

I loved my friends who good-naturedly teased me.

I loved that rain which made me cling to him,

I loved that moment which sealed my fate with him.

They often ask me, "Who then is your Valentine?"

A question that amuses and puzzles me all the time.

But as my true being has evolved by those people, things, events, and time,

Hence together they can sum up to be my Valentine.

20. My Telephonic Romance

When she coyly holds the receiver,

And her fingers gently play with its cords,

I know that I am in her thoughts today,

A reason to cheer a lot!

When she does not answer the phone in the first
ring,

But answers it anyway, in the fifth or the sixth ring
taking her own sweet time,

I know that she is playing hard to get today,

And expects me to chase her sometimes.

When she picks the landline,

But answers in court, formal 'yes' or ' no' mode,

I know that she is displeased with me today,

And only my genuine efforts can renew our
informal code.

When she rings me at the office at odd hours,

Which she usually evades at other days,

I know that in her own way she is pointing out today that,

No rules could be applied in her case.

When she holds the receiver tightly in her hands,

And whisper sweet nothings in my ear,

I know that she is in love with me,

And includes me in her prayers.

21. The Mermaids' Ramp

The humongous island in the faraway sea had a
scandalous stamp,

The veteran sailors aptly named it 'The
Mermaids' Ramp'.

For the blue-eyed beauties called the mermaids,
with their luscious lips,

Heaved their bare, heavy breasts as they spotted a
ship.

The sailors who dared to answer the beckoning
seductresses,

Found themselves to be carried away by their
chosen enchantresses.

Next, on the island, they were sent to an alluring
trance,

And the sexy sirens entertained them with a
seductive dance.

In their foolhardiness, as they tried to have coitus
with their femme fatale,

A sudden, treacherous feeling would warn them
that all was not well.

And before they could fully comprehend that they were caught in a vicious trap,

The Mermaids' sharp fangs would tear their fleshes in half.

With their wild, terrified eyes, the nearly departed souls would behold,

That the golden, curly-haired, ravishing mermaids did not have a heart of gold.

Their ears would record their own dirge song,

Which the mermaids mockingly sang to them while feasting along.

And as they were done eating the sailors, licking their lips,

They began to wait again, with patience, for the next passing ship.

For they knew that their prey humans had a taste for lust,

It was their Achilles heel, which would bring them to dust.

B.

Hues of Life

1. O Life, Colour Me with Your Hues

O life, color me with your hues,

Let me get drenched amidst them.

Inspire me by being my muse,

To explore and love every bit of your realm.

Let me get lost in your lush greeneries,

Let me feel your mesmerizing sceneries,

Let me take a trip to forbidden, forsaken lands,

Let me get immersed in sojourns unplanned.

Let me laugh a little,

And cry a little more,

Let me hear echoes of my voice,

And make a boisterous uproar.

Let me fall in love,

With a pristine heart,

Let me feel my presence,

In another beating heart.

Let me face my failures,

Let me face my punishments,

Let me know what needs to be known,

About scars, sorrows, and bereavement.

Let my hopes be lifted,

Let my hopes be crushed,

Let me gain the knowledge of,

'Who', 'how', and 'what'.

Let me sing a little,

Let me dance with joyous abandon,

Let me whisper sweet nothings to my love,

In a soft, melodious tone.

Let me be colored with all your hues,

Let me experience your full cycle with pride,

Please let me discover myself,

While walking your paths with a smile.

2. The Song of Life

Succulent life,

Bestowing bitter-sweet portions of,

Unique, unsullied moments,

Set the tune of that song,

Which would unfailingly determine,

How we would lead this life,

And where we would belong.

Our busy-idle days,

Our escaping getaways,

Our love, hate, and wrongs,

Each of our actions would contribute in its way,

To enrich our life's song.

And as we reflect on,

Our perjuries, prejudices, and purgation,

Our hopes, dreams, and ambitions,

We surely would find in this world our place,

That the song of our life has allotted to us,

To accept with grace.

3. The City

Intrepid dreams, beckoning the rooted, giving them a thousand reasons,

To prepare themselves to be uprooted.

Now begin their nomadic tales,

In the city life, echoing their silent screams,

A price which must be paid dearly to this 'Charon',

To pass his river Styx.

The undercurrents of tension, despair, and for that matter failure,

Should not deter the city-bound journey of,

The swarming locusts called mortals.

And as such the city, like a true enchantress,

Adorns itself in its best attire,

That is, the lights grandiose,

To bedazzle and to make one feel that he is uprooted,

For a better cause, for a noble purpose.

And what then follows is a hackneyed tale,

The locusts encircling themselves around the alluring lights,

Some live, some die, and some flee realizing the trap.

But the best-kept secret is that they would return,

This time grooming themselves to fit in, to win,

In other words, they would return with a better stratagem.

4. The Song of Life

As he saw the sleep-deprived, blood-shot eyes of his comrades,

And watched their tired legs,

Almost refusing to obey to move one inch more,

He did what he does best,

He sang their tribes that spirited song,

To make them remember how far they had come along.

The best news was that they had survived.

Oh, yes! They had survived,

The indiscriminate killings,

The harsh cold weather, the slave-bound life and

the bloody lootings.

And since then, they had just run and walked,

Walked, and ran, crossing miles and miles,

Like hunted animals of some kind,

Frightened and lost, praying to their heathen gods,

To help them just to survive from their fate unkind.

And had left their known territories, their loved ones' lifeless bodies,

Scattered in the bloodied alleys near their broken huts.

He knew that now they must go on,

For life will rekindle again only if they survive this game.

And then they could again dream and plan to win back their now-conquered homeland,

To win back their much-revered ancestor's hills and plains.

And who knows,

One day they might even be strong enough,

To conquer and annex their enemy terrains!

But all these would be possible only if their life remains!

And so, he sang that spirited song,

So that they could move on with long strides,

To climb that one last hill,

To meet life,

To embrace a new dawn.

5. Dear Life...

Dear life,

Sometimes, you had thrown me to the wolves,

For reasons unknown,

And tested my resilience.

Put my back on the wall,

By throttling my confidence,

And highlighted my disarrayed face.

Put me on trial,

For crimes not committed,

And exiled me to an abysmal state of mind.

Plotted revenge for deeds,

Which though done with fair intention by me
had gone horribly wrong,

And thus charred my lively heart.

Forestalled my triumph,

Which could have otherwise brought my
salvation,

By coaxing me to do self-defeating acts.

Misled me,

When I needed guidance most,

And bloodied my feet on the path of thorns.

And yet, and yet,

I hold you dear in my heart,

As you have taught me,

To play this unfair game with aplomb,

And savor the occasional slices of happiness.

6. Paper Boats

As the year's first rains from the heavens,

Slacken its pace,

The young, excited faces of the neighborhoods,

Braces themselves, for their paper boat race.

The multi-colored boats,

Represent multi-colored dreams that,

Only a child could weave with his imagination of rainbow threads.

An adult, with his understanding of life would,

Fail to resonate with it,

As he is a sinner, who has seen too much,

A victim, who has tasted his share of the twists of time, experience, chance, and fate.

The soft breeze,

As if with an intention to tease,

Caresses the tender corner of the boats,

Giving a fillip to their speed.

And their owners run with them,

Emulating the pirates of the ocean,

Risking everything, as if to seek some hidden treasures without fail.

The cherubic faces, whether of fair,

Brown, pale, or black complexion,

All together become red with anticipation,

As their boats crisscrossing all the barriers of mud,

Small mounds of garbage or pebbles,

Dumped in the overflowing drains,

Almost reach their destination.

And as the winning boat touches the line of victory,

Its disheveled hair, the five-year-old winner gives,

An intense dance of exhilaration whose moves seem exclusive his own.

And viewing it, everybody knows that,

In this first race of life, he has gallantly won.

7. Let My Lies Prevail

Can I claim that the lies of my life,

Have soiled my heart?

Or have they restored hope,

To initiate a refreshing start?

Will I ditch my lies,

And embrace my raw truths?

Or will I let go of the truths,

A friend so uncouth?

Are my lies beguiling, bewitching,

My desired alternative tale?

Or are they my chosen weapon,

To muffle my inner wails?

Are those dreams, woven around my lies,

Should be uprooted at the first chance?

Or will I sustain them a little,

To perform an ecstatic dance?

Have my lies impeded my growth,

Derailed my life's focus?

Or have they liberated me,

From my painful past?

The thing is, my friends, I am a bit in love with my lies.

As they may not be rewarding, but they shower respite.

For I am not a knight in quest of the holy grail -

So, let me live a little bit, let my lies prevail.

8. Rewinding Life

What should I rewind?

My untold miserable state of mind?

Or that sudden surge of love blind?

My scandalous freefall from the palace of
illusions?

Or my rapid, existential practical solutions?

My tethered, unspoken, immolated self?

Or my coming of age with my loved ones' help?

Those ceaseless moments of undiluted pain?

Or my unabashed dance at the music of rain?

My beaten, battered state, in the face of
adversity?

Or my soulful search for balance and sanity?

Those punishing moments when it really did
hurt?

Or those cherished moments when I was spoiled
rotten with love?

Those dilly-dallying, nerve-wracking phases of
indecision?

Or my walking the long road of life to
comprehend realism?

As I look back at my life with some regret and
some hope,

I get a bird's eye view of my life's broad-spectrum
bioscope.

Here the bigger picture is scripted with my
inaction, action, pains, and gain,

So, if I have to rewind, I guess,

I have to give equal weightage to all of them.

9. So, Can You Hear Me?

I have crash-landed,

In the abysmal quicksand of my sins.

It is now devouring me little by little,

Sans mercy, sans redemption.

The gossamer of lies that I had spun throughout my life,

Had long ago shaken the ground beneath my feet.

And the megalomaniac in me,

Had further spiraled the antithesis of trust, love, and hope in my life.

I had bullied and battered,

Shaken and shattered the trusting ones.

And now, like a tired and petrified lone ranger,

Desperately seeking one kind smile, one trusting face.

I had half smiled, half cried, half lived, half loved,

Always keeping the other half for scrutiny.

But had always hated fully with hell-bent stubbornness,

Puking vengeance even on understandably unintentional slights.

Still, the mirage of hope keeps appearing,

Flickering my wish to do things right this time.

The crash couldn't crush this one final wish to be heard, for a second chance.

So, can you hear me?

10. Stateless

The UN had tried to negotiate with,

The warring trespassers.

But alas! As anticipated,

The negotiations failed.

The morsel of land,

That we, now, the refugees, had,

Known as our homeland for centuries,

Now belonged to them.

Now 'they' could be anyone,

Their religion undoubtedly would be the
machine guns.

Their violence would put to shame,

Even the scriptural depiction of infernal flames.

They only knew the language of coercion,

In fact, anything but reason,

Anything that would,

Reiterate their unjust claims.

Sometimes religious apartheid,

Sometimes unholy crusaders of state had,

Rendered millions, like us, homeless.

We were sentenced to suffer,

A stateless state of mind-

To wander eternally on the brink of insanity,

While coming to terms with the fact that,

We were godforsaken creatures,

Destined to remain stateless throughout our remaining lives.

11. Time's Gift

Time stood still the moment,

He locked his lips with mine,

And crushed me in his heart.

Time stood still the moment,

I hold my little one in hand,

And touched his rosy cheeks.

Time stood still the moment,

My boy first called me 'ma',

And laughed at my amazement.

Time stood still the moment,

I believed that since I have him,

Now I can do wonders.

They say time waits for none and flies for ever.

But I guess, it sprinkles such moments that we can savor.

These moments remain etched in our minds,

Making our journey bliss of a kind.

12. Time's Tentacles

Time,

Gargantuan, omnipotent, omniscient, omnipresent,

Armored with its ticking tentacles,

Embark upon its mission to catch up with us,

'The fallible.'

Its pace though neither slow nor fast,

Must ensure a rhythmic, methodical regularity,

For its quest to collect the granules of its sands from us,

Must have the stamp of impartiality.

The full cycle of this life of ours,

With all its myriad hues,

Our emergence, prominence, and decadence,

Everything is impeccably recorded in its ticking jurisprudence.

It unfailingly veers the course of our journey,

By slowly unraveling the roles assigned to us by fate.

And we must play it or retire 'when it's time,'

By keeping in mind, the date.

All our joys, success, pain, and loss,

Everything that we have come across clockwise,

Must be returned before our final departure
without fail,

Under the careful supervision of time's ever-
vigilant eyes.

This all-time incumbent navigator of those
legendary wheels of time,

Takes upon itself to portray the role of an
iconoclast,

To put an end to our narcissistic, over-glorified
selves,

By finally transforming us, the mere mortals to
dust.

13. Nostalgia

Somethings remain,

Inked in your heart,

That has jolted you,

Somehow, somewhere.

It stays with you,

As a balm or a pain,

And becomes something,

Called nostalgia.

Your nostalgic self,

Rejoices and grieves,

Pines and screams,

Maybe for that lost love,

First kiss,

Or your native land.

A sweet pain,

Engulfs your being,

As an old picture, a similar place,

A known person or a used thing,

Makes you reconstruct,

Those events again,

In your brain.

Nostalgia reminds you,

From time to time,

That those sweet nothings,

Those crushed dreams,

Those life-changing decisions,

Or your silent screams,

All has become a part of your present self.

You have lived life,

For better or worse,

But you must come to terms,

With your evolved self.

14. The Books That Had Shaped My Life

Amidst the old books stacked haphazardly,

At the bookcase in my dilapidated ancestral home,

Amidst those dusty avenues of wisdom,

I could still trace back my footprints,

As their yellowish, mildewed pages had impeccably fossilized,

My childhood finger imprints.

Touched, I navigated through them again,

First, by just carefully turning those pages,

And soon by engaging again in reading those gems.

This time, I did it not to know the stories,

Or to gain the wisdom they offer,

But simply to revisit my childhood companions,

Who had given me so much,

Without asking much but a little bit of my time.

Those books had borne testimony of,

My first moments of awakening and had

Tried to quench a little girl's thirst to know almost everything.

They were instrumental in imbibing in me,

A lifelong passion to assimilate events and

To synchronize every step of my life with learning.

Before leaving, as I again put them in the bookcase there,

This time I did it neatly and with great care,

For they were the books that had shaped my life and

Like true friends, taught me to love, care, and share.

15. Mahatma

His journey began,

Amidst a diffident, defeated nation,

Shackled for two hundred years,

By the colossal colonial rulers,

Called the British.

His vision of freedom,

For his countrymen were,

Mocked, jeered at,

By that despotic lot, who,

Attempted to trifle his acts,

Stating it as 'gibberish'.

But he stood tall,

On those dark days,

Introducing non-violence,

And peaceful ways,

Reawakening the inner strength of his people's resolution.

In time, his ways would,

Crush the almost impenetrable walls of bondage,

And history would witness and

Record a free nation's ascension.

But it was not mere independence,

Which he handed over to his nation.

There was something more,

In his dream and his vision.

And that was,

His attempt to teach his countrymen,

To constantly strive for non-violence and peace.

And that's what makes him 'Mahatma',

To his nation and to the world,

Which often seems so divided,

Engaging in trivialities.

16. My Poems Matters

The influx of random, scandalous, marvelous
thoughts and ideas,

Raising an alarming pandemonium in the deepest
recesses of my being,

Almost coerce me to hold my pen to write
poems,

About this, that, and everything.

I feel that my pen must write,

About my deeply layered ideas and thoughts,

What I know is felt by everyone,

But what they are unable to meaningfully record.

I am blessed and privileged,

To be a poet who can churn words,

And I arrange those words as meaningful verses,

And these verses are designed to paint my and
others' inner universe.

I am sure all would read my poems and laugh
and bleed with me,

As it would surely echo their inner dreams and
silent screams,

My poems would be an instrument of their
empowerment,

As here, they would discover their relatable,
inner realm.

17. Camera Moments

In our imperfect, time-bound existence,

Precious moments pass without much resistance.

The ticking bomb called time turns the young to old,

And the reminiscing souls lament that there is so much to be told.

Hence the camera becomes us that visual storyteller,

The time machine swapping present for a bygone era.

A perfect device to churn tales of perfect moments,

Bringing smiles, and tears of gratitude with its captured fragments.

Photos with family, friends, neighbors, and colleagues,

The living and the dead become personal relics.

It is something that provides that much-needed soothing touch,

As it documents how we have lived and how we have been loved.

The heartbreaks of life take a backseat it seems,

As the cherished photos weaves a world of dreams.

The captured moments give us an emotional high,

As it teaches us to celebrate the event called life.

18. Memories of Happiness

Those deeply buried memories of my past,

Tip-toed back to me, as I sat restlessly in my armchair,

Sleep-deprived, on that cold winter night.

It felt as if those long-past events were happening there and then,

In that shivering, cold realm,

And the characters from my past seemed perfectly playing along,

In that little nocturnal game.

To begin with,

I saw that girl from my childhood days,

Who used to pass the lane near my house almost every day,

In her bicycle, sucking her popsicle,

Every time throwing me that inviting smile,

As if beseeching me with it to join her to cover a few flower-filled miles.

Then I saw that boy,

Whose name I could not recall now,

The son of our house help,

Who, wearing his same dirty black striped pant
and an oversized shirt,

Used to come to our home with her mother and
used to sit in a remote corner,

Not minding the surrounding dirt.

He used to finish his meal with a lightning speed,

And then with immense happiness used to
showcase his disco feats,

Leaving everyone in splits,

Embarrassing his mother with his 'disco-
misdeeds.'

Those memories of mine of that boy and that
girl,

Those priceless moments of happiness with my
childhood pals,

Cured my restlessness that night,

And soon sleep embraced me in her arms,

Endowing me with its magic potion of happiness,
peace, and calm.

19. Mother-An Eternal Soul

The unbeaten souls called our mothers,

Complete us, their fallible offspring,

With their magic potion of love and

By always believing in us, with the same
sentiment,

Same feelings.

They are undeterred, unstoppable,

In relentlessly pursuing their primary goal,

To gift the very best of everything to us,

Without thinking much,

About their own welfare as such.

The unalloyed love that spring,

From these fountains of love,

Rescue us from the burning flames,

That tries to devour us,

As we collide with various volcanic eruptions,

While engaging ourselves in life's unfair games.

After each defeat, we choose not to retreat,

But gather the pieces of our shattered selves,

To begin again,

As we are taught to do so,

By our first teacher, our mothers,

To not to give in without a proper fight,

Not to give in until the end of the game.

They are the carriers of hope,

Instilling the same in us drop by drop.

For they are our mothers, the eternal souls,

Connecting us with this universe whole,

Sometimes with their umbilical cord and

Sometimes, by becoming the beacon light,

Guiding us towards our chosen goals.

Note: I dedicate this poem to my mother
Mrs.Kakali Chowdhury, who is the biggest
inspiration of my life.

20. Maa

Her bold eyes welcomed my bald head amidst yells and pain,

A totally round creature with a toothless mouth became her summer rain.

Amidst conscious, semi-conscious and unconscious state she yearned for my ugly sweet being,

Thinking that only she knew the magic to transform me to some Disney queen.

Determined to create something meaningful out of that total mess,

She buckled up herself fully to face her massive test.

With fierce love and pure heart, she prioritised my needs and wants,

An enduring, repetitive daily task with no guarantees and P.F funds.

She cajoled my father to put me in a reputed school,

And pretended to manage the fees and other paraphernalia with a total cool.

But I knew that the financial part with its endless claws had given her goosebumps,

For I witnessed her making deals with her God with prayers and endless chants.

In an effort to ease her mind, I told her my own aim,

I, then a little girl, promised to become a household name.

She believed me fully and never doubted my resolution,

It seemed that her ugly duckling was finally reaching her destination.

Her sarees were ordinary, and her meals were simple,

I never found her having her eyes on some expensive jewel.

But I can tell you that real sadness used to engulf her otherwise happy being,

At occasions when she detected lackadaisical attitude in me or my sibling.

She defined us as her 'heart' and 'pulse' with a
soaring delight,

Ever ready to make amends in us by putting up
an energetic fight.

She knew no feminism and never fought for her
own rights,

Her only dream was that her' heart' and 'pulse'
get a meaningful life.

Years later, the cycle of life brought her to the
stage of old age,

And I did not become that household name as I
promised in my tender age.

I am not ashamed though, as thanks to her, I
carved my own path,

By giving others boundless, uncalculated love.

21. How to Make a Perfect Christmas Dough (List Poetry)

First in a large clean bowl of winter-laden December,

Put several heaps of snow,

Mix it well with a pinch of stars,

To make a Christmas dough.

Next add ten full cups of reindeer sleighs' delightful 'jingle bell' sound,

And a bucket of Santas knocking doors,

Shake it well before marinating it further with a spoonful of Christmas Carol singers,

To make a soft Christmas dough.

As it softens now, pour a bottle of children's happiness,

And two three drops of their handmade snowman's radiant glow,

To sweeten it further, pour a can of their boisterous laughter,

To make a Christmas dough.

Now is the time to include in it a quintal of your
prayers,

And a kilo of your new year resolutions and
vows,

Roll it nicely with a gallon of our Lord's blessings,

To make a perfect Christmas dough.

Now shape the dough like one sky full of dreams,

Or shape it like a series of red brigade devotees
praying in rows,

Now put it in the hot oven of belief for a few
minutes,

Before bringing out the baked Christmas dough.

Now garnish it with a hundred socks of cake,

cookies, candies, presents, and turkey roasts,

And a generous sprinkling of Christmas trees'
wish-come-true boughs,

Also don't forget to sprinkle a little number of
bedecked wreaths and illuminated, throbbing-
with life-streets,

Before distributing all a piece of your delectable
baked Christmas dough.

C.

Peekaboo!

1. The Child Within Me

The child within me refuses to bid adieu,

To the exotic feeling of wonder,

Which it receives while navigating its milieu.

It sings and dances,

Engaging in pure romance,

While viewing something as simple as,

The giant leap of a grasshopper,

Or something as marvellous as the constellation
of stars.

It gets overwhelmed while listening,

To the songs of a solitary reaper,

Or while observing the sonorous flow,

Of a nameless brook or a renowned river.

This child unleashes in me an unbridled passion,

To live this life with hopes and ambitions,

To dream big and to nurture a broader vision,

To unite all by erasing division.

It fuels me with an Epicurean scholar's fire,

Whisper me to get bathed in hedonistic desires,

Inspire me to soar higher,

To greet life in all its colours.

It dreams to touch the lapis lazuli sky,

To meet a hyacinth girl by travelling miles,

To breathe excitement by revelling with
flamboyance and style,

And finally, to celebrate the event called life.

2. I Am Still a Child at Heart

In my mind, the sky still retains the mysteries of
the universe,

The rain still evokes that thirst for dance,

The weepy willows still give me the jitters,

And the flowers still seem to throw me their
playful glance.

I can still feel the pulse of nature,

Still manage to smile back at the smiling faces,

Still manage to sing a song or two impromptus,

And eat sweets guilt-free without fretting over
tooth decay.

I still manage to feel blessed for my mere
existence,

Still believe in peaceful co-existence,

Still happy with sweet nothings,

And still sometimes cry over trifle things.

I still rely on the stars for miracles,

I can still calmly speak about my life's debacle.

I still play hide-and -seek with life,

I still put lipstick, mascaras with pride.

I still seek answers for questions,

I still work to leave a mark,

I still have the courage to fail,

And the courage to get hurt.

I am not a know-all fool,

I am still learning the art of living,

My heart still beats,

In accordance with life's maddening rhythm.

I am not a chubby cheek nor a blue eye,

But am a child too,

Living life by practicing,

The life principles of a child.

D.

Let There Be Light!

1. The Dreams of My Heart (Janaku)

Dreams,

Heathen, pagan,

Captivating my soul.

Dancing

Attuned with

Melodies of renaissance.

Portraying,

A gargantuan,

Universe of subalterns.

Forever,

Championing the

Ideas truly modern.

Beckoning

Me so

That I breathe.

Amidst

Freshly brewed,

Love laced breeze.

Producing,

Soft, rhythmic,

Waves of tintinnabulations.

With,

Its spontaneous

Overflow of ministrations.

Making

My metamorphosis

As a brave heart.

By

Forever listening

Melodies of heart.

2. The She Saga

Finally, the rendezvous has begun,

In our very own Hall of Fame,

Where we would rightfully channelize our own flames,

To create, re-create new wholes,

And embrace new roles.

It is a place where,

We would have a date with ourselves,

Where we could paint, sing, dance, and dress,

Even could create a mess,

And still would not be embarrassed of,

Our own vulnerable selves.

What's more,

Here every time we would be embraced,

With a true-smiling face.

Now we are a part of this tribe,

The stinging bees of this honey-filled hive.

Here we would push our own boundaries,

To again reclaim our lost territories.

And give strength to each other's cause,

By building bridges,

So, that no one feels lost.

We would compose,

The songs and symphonies of our own 'ragas'.

For we have earned this place with our own love,

We have finally arrived in the She Saga.

3. My Dear Girl, You Must Know...

My dear girl, you must know,

That the storms of calamity could,

Make your pace of progress slow.

The lightnings of despair could fall with all its might,

And you might spend many sleepless nights.

The promises made to you could fail.

And in pursuit of heaven, you might end up in hell!

He who would promise you love, could change his mind,

And you might suffer for his words unkind.

Those whom you trust, might conspire against you,

And you could be beaten black and blue!

The winters could be bitter cold and the summers piping hot,

And you could be alienated and left to rot!

Your steps might falter, and your dreams could be shattered,

And you might be judged for words not uttered!

So, my girl, you must know that,

You must have the guts,

To survive these blows.

Only then, with time, you would know,

How to run and even steal this show.

4. Unfulfilled Dream

Fate did brandish its sword,

For a long time, to intimidate me,

Sabotaging my numerous noble efforts,

To realize my unfulfilled dream,

To break free.

I was pushed, I was shoved,

And countless catastrophes,

Attempted to crush,

My rebellious being.

But then fate gave in,

When it tasted my resilience.

And even showered me,

With a thoughtful parting gift.

And that was,

To have the strength and spirit,

To break free,

Thus fulfilling,

My long unfulfilled dream.

5. My Life's Learning

I did mind when the vicious quagmire of illusions,

Scorched the lush meadows of my heart.

I did wail when I accidently slipped,

Into the murky, pungent-smelling pond of greed,

And lost myself by drowning in it with lightning speed.

I did scream when the gossamer of lies,

Slowly unravelled its nefarious plans to take away my innocence,

And persistently mocked my resilience,

To rescue myself from my own decadence.

I almost dutifully failed in that venture called love,

When my beloved squandered my most precious investment, my heart,

Without thinking much of its consequences upon me as such.

And then I frantically knocked at the wrong doors, took the wrong turns,

Hoping to salvage myself from that hurt.

My purgation began when I fearlessly immersed myself,

To comprehend the myriad hues of life.

And soon I realized that all those above-mentioned events were,

A part of the complex syllabus of life.

As that realization dawned upon me,

I then patiently awaited the arrival of the blazing rays of truth.

Soon it arrived piercingly all myths,

Nullifying all lies uncouth.

Those illusions could no longer now trespass there at my heart,

As by now I was forged as a true survivor who could totally knock them out.

I again began to live my life,

But this time brewing hope and happiness,

In this age-old saga of struggle and strife.

6. Letters of Parvati

Once I had opened our wooden curved 'treasure box',

A family heirloom, that had remained with us for generations.

There, amidst the potpourri of different things,

I happened to find some letters,

Fastened with a black ribbon, which caught my fascination.

While getting the joy of reading them,

I also got a glimpse of the life of their writer, one 'Parvati',

And the incidents that had led her to write them,

To my great-grandmother 'Gauri', who happened to be her childhood friend.

In one of the letters, after the then fifteen-year-old bride Parvati,

Lost her twenty-year senior husband to cholera, she wrote,

"I have lost nothing Gauri as he had never loved me.

I was just his housekeeper, whom he had married
for a hefty sum of dowry.

The best part is, I am not doomed to spend the
rest of my life in his memory.

I would live, I would fight,

And would do something good with my life."

In another letter, I sensed a change of tone,

As an eighteen- year -old Parvati wrote that,

She had fallen for one 'Mohan'.

"I think I am in love, my friend.

It seems I do nothing but to wait for him,

Ever eager to fulfil his every whim!

And the best part is that he loves me too!

That day, near the pond, he whispered at my
ears, I love you."

The final letter of the twenty-year old,

Explained her distress manifold,

"They are sending me to Kashi, Gauri,

Banishing me to the ghetto of widows.

There, my head would be shaved and

I would be taught how to 'behave'.

The best part is...

No, this time there is no best part my friend.

This time, I have no choice but to live a life of lies,

As a devoted devotee of our gods upright.

I have been robbed of my love, of my life,

And they claim it is the only path to save a widow's soul,

From falling for worldly delights."

7. Wonder Woman's Appraisal of the Superwomen of this World

I have heard on the grapevine that, I, the Wonder Woman,

Brainchild of the Marvel comics department is,

Winning serious accolades, worldwide.

All men seem to drool over me,

Well! That's natural, as I am endowed with beauty, brains, and superpowers, you see!

The critics have discovered a New Woman in me,

And my fans, men, and women alike wonder,

How could I perform such Herculean tasks in a jiffy!

But though I am eulogized and celebrated here,

For my superwoman traits, I must say that,

The female mortals of this globe have remained,

Widely ignorant about their own superpowers, till date.

And their male counterparts?

Well, they are more than ignorant, you see,

As they are adding insult to injury,

By playing the role of supercilious judge and jury!

What about that acid- attack survivor girl,

Who lost everything in a moment and still chose
to live with dignity?

Or, that dark-skinned underprivileged girl,

Who opposed early marriage and decided to
study even amid abject poverty?

Would you not hail that rape victim,

Who refused to remain silent and told in a
packed courtroom,

The 'shameful' details of that harrowing incident?

Or, what about that woman who suffered and
survived domestic abuse, and

Still remained unbeaten?

These are only few instances of such
superwomen, you see,

And how their stories remain unheard and
unappreciated, still amazes me!

Mortals! You don't need a Supergirl from a
different world to take an inspiration,

Just give a good look at your own world, which, I truly believe, is a superwoman's creation.

8. Tale of a Transwoman

The labyrinth with its menacing mazes loomed large in her mind,

Ready to devour her silent screams.

She sighed, as she had always known it,

That one day they would surely stampede,

Her cherished inner coherent world of sanity and dreams.

For she had bloomed as a transwoman,

Disrupting the balance of their 'natural' realm.

Now as she was discovered,

They had her back against the wall.

And an exorcism would be performed upon her,

To make her fit into their version of 'normal'.

Her choices would now be stifled,

Her voice would now be muffled,

Leaving no chance for her to resurrect her true self.

9. Diary of a 'Different' Girl

She was demeaned,

Belittled everywhere,

For her chosen sexuality.

She knew that it was her fate,

To be mocked or laughed at,

By this herd mentality.

For she had come out openly,

To declare her metamorphosis,

From her male to a female form.

Yes, she was a transgender,

And proud for,

Making her chosen transform.

She was looked down upon,

Heard baseless assumptions,

And was the butt of various jokes.

She faced queries like,

"Are you normal?", "how do you do 'that'?

From insensitive, jeering folks.

Her friends, playmates, colleagues from work,

Now watch her,

With narrow, suspicious eyes.

The whole neighbourhood,

Declared her in unison,

An evil witch with ominous ties.

Even her loved ones,

Had chosen to banish her,

After hearing her 'season of change'.

Her parents angrily ordered her,

To leave the house,

For embracing an idea so strange!

But she had known from her little life,

That nothing lasts forever,

Not even the scornful boos of the crowd.

She had left it to time,

To heal her wounds,

And chose not to protest aloud.

10. Dear Face book Girl...

The fb (face book) girl in her fb world is sharing her radiant smile,

The fb girl in her real world is supressing her painful sigh.

The fb girl in her fb world pens her romantic tale,

The fb girl in her real world is sensing her romance to fade.

The fb girl in her fb world is sharing her pouts while boarding a plane,

The fb girl in her real world is running away from her known terrain.

The fb girl in her fb world is sharing Sadguru's wisdom,

The fb girl in her real world is suffering from acute depression.

The fb world in her fb world is thanking all for 1.2k likes,

The fb girl in her real world is a victim of meanness and dislike.

The fb girl in her fb world is lauded for having a brilliant mind,

The fb girl in her real world is ostracized for being one of a kind.

The fb girl in her fb world is winning the online diva contest,

The fb girl in her real world is stamped as her family's disgrace.

The fb girl in her fb world is putting up a brave face,

The fb girl in her real world is losing her happy space.

Let's forgive the girl's dilemma as she is in a conflicting phase,

She is a product of a world which isolates the scarred faces.

The fb girl has webbed her fb world to conceal her pains and scars,

It is a desperate attempt from her side to win her loosing war.

The fb girl in her fb avatar gives every New Woman delight,

Let's pray our fb girl wins her actual fight.

11. My Menstruation Story

I bled,

Like a true specimen of my tribe,

To be in sync with my world which believed,

'She who bleeds is a lust and fecund garden of our Eden,'

'For she will procreate for us like a true woman.'

I religiously bled in all the months of all the coming years,

Enduring nausea, low spirit, weakness, and abdominal pain,

Keeping in mind those 'golden' words,

That I had to bled to become a true woman.

In my world, I was denied sanitary pads,

For it was expensive, they concluded.

They supplied me rags instead,

Which many times got me infected.

For those five days of every month of every year,

They coerced me to participate in the touch-me-
not game,

Like an untouchable, I was barred from touching
my Gods,

For I was 'impure' then, they claimed.

It was always a hush hush affair,

Not to be fairly discussed in the family drawing
room,

My grandma endeavoured to douse my
adolescent rage by stating,

"Why girl, it is much better now.

In our times by now they would have found you a
groom!"

They took it upon themselves to make me a
woman by degrees,

For now, that I was bleeding, I could not be set
free.

I was schooled to guard my chastity at every cost,

Which meant less freedom, more boundaries,
and more stumbling blocks.

So, I bled without much choice,

I bled by losing my voice.

Instead, I was burdened with inhibitions by them,

And I lost my simple self while playing their
unfair game.

They say menstruation in many ways is a
liberating experience,

As with its beginning a girl touches the threshold
of womanhood in her adolescence.

I suppose it happens to other girls in other
worlds.

But the multi-hues of the season of change
remained unattainable to me.

Now I know for sure that I was told to bleed for
all the wrong reasons,

For not only my body but also my heart bled in
all those gruesome seasons.

12. Greetings To All Women!

Greetings to all women for being instrumental,

In portraying a picture of a brave new world,

Which would run on the wheels of,

Courage, liberty, equality, and love.

Greetings to them for showing resilience while facing vicissitudes of life,

For showing resilience while giving voice to their common cause,

And for dreaming to hand over posterity a bed of roses.

Greetings to them for attempting to rewrite their destiny,

By erasing the stigma of being called the 'second sex',

And for endeavouring to veer,

The course of their miserable lives towards a smooth sail.

Greetings to them for achieving the milestone of being 'heard',

And for providing opportunities to their tribe,

For redressal of their grievances at all costs.

Greetings to them for popularizing the concept of
'choice',

And for attempting to vindicate the rights of
women by making the right noise.

Finally, greetings to them for their hope,

To win all battles in the long run,

Which would brighten our lives,

With the brightness of a thousand splendid suns.

Note: While writing this poem, I have taken
inspiration from Simone de Beauvoir's 'The
Second Sex', Mary Wollstonecraft's 'Vindication
of the Rights of Woman' and from Khaled
Hosseini's novel 'A Thousand Splendid Suns'.

13. Prometheus Unbound

For a long time, my misfit soul,

Couldn't rock and roll-

As it was chained, fettered, misjudged, and misspent,

By those, who relished,

To decree punishments upon souls,

Who, like it, nurtured avant-garde ideas,

And aspired to create luminous halos of their own.

For a long time, my misfit soul,

Couldn't rock and roll,

As it was banished to the infamous dungeon of loneliness,

And its key was thrown into the boundless sea.

There, like a career criminal,

It was punished to wait,

For its own apocalypse,

By dreading a bleak future, by dreading a dark 'unknown'.

But it did the Herculean task of breaking the shackles,

By smashing the rusted, outdated, predictable lock,

Which had, for so long kept it bound.

And it soared high, like Daedalus,

By mending its two broken wings-

As long ago, it had resolved to find the key to freedom,

To become mankind's first Prometheus Unbound.

E.

Grazing the Meadows of Nature

1. The Redeemer Night

As the thaumaturge night,

Dissolved the chamber of evanescent clouds
hitherto obfuscating the sky,

She now had an uncluttered view of her own
intrepid dreams,

Reflecting in its silvery effulgent smile.

A saccharine music ensued,

Amidst the effervescent celestial figures,

Evoking a state of ebullience within her.

But she then reminisced about how she once,

Endeavored to conquer the frozen hearts,

Who fed in her weakness,

And rejoiced as she plummeted down in the
vicious quagmire of darkness.

She remembered, how she was once gaslighted,

Ending up questioning her own reasons.

That resultant pandemonium within her then
almost caused her doom,

And she stood alone bereft of empathy in all
those gruesome seasons.

This time, the night being cognizant of her
scarred past,

Decided to become her redeemer and kept
siding with her dreams.

The stars kept wayfaring with her as her knights
in armour,

Illuminating her path, with a generous dose of
their sacrosanct light.

The glowworms alighted on her to
metamorphose her as a magical being,

While the passing breeze enthralled everyone
with its mellifluous singing.

The exotic aroma of the hasnahanas,

Further resplended the milieu,

Rendering that quintessential essence in the air to
usher something new.

Hence, her granules of wisdom now derived
from,

These eclectic potpourris of sights, sounds, and
smells.

Her pagan heart now soared high,

To blend with the equilibrium of the wise stars,

Thus, creating new dimensions to know herself.

Her talisman, the night made her unsullied soul
to respond,

To the unalloyed love, magic, and music
orchestrated by the cosmos.

And she, now a stardust soul, could render,

Cosmic vibes in all purposes.

And lo! Everything seemed new in that
enlightened night!

It was as if it groomed her for an upcoming
joyous ride of her life.

2. Ode to Spring

The verdant viridescence now refurbishes nature,

Who not so long ago was besieged by cold and
distant winter.

And just as then her look of vast stretch of white
nothingness was unmissable,

So is now her floral apparel.

The past dirge now gives way to epithalamium of
the senses,

And the banquet opens for the seasonal
jamboree.

The bisou of life is palpable everywhere,

As new leaves again grace the hitherto forlorn
branches of seemingly despondent trees.

The metamorphosis could be further traced,

In the chirping ditties of the soaring pagan hearts,
or

In the scenes of comely, almost melodious
bucolic noon, or by simply

Beholding the vast canopy of the lapis lazuli sky.

The freshly brewed breeze transfers its warmth,

In the soft carpet of the budding blades of grass.

And as the heathen blooms waltzes in joyous
abandon,

An enchanting fragrance percolates in the length
and breadth of this exotic kingdom.

While the relentless buzzing sound echoes
around the surrounding,

The grasshoppers hop revelling in their trifle
findings.

The butterflies, steeped in the hues of this colour
carnival,

Glide past one beauty to other sans caring for
approval.

The potpourri of sight, smell, and sounds,

Builds up a succulent life, which would remain
now for the time being.

And the magic and the music reach its crescendo,

With this liberal dose of vernal offerings.

3. Summer's Last Lament

Adios for now! I am adjourning my session to make way for monsoon,

Suspending the ceaseless fusillade of my blazing rays.

In short, I would not besmirch my good name,

By elongating this sizzling hot game!

My only grouse is that my viridescent warm summer fields seem so bereft,

After being denied the golden touch of those small, tireless, running feet.

Is it true then that their obsession with gadgets has become their nemesis?

It is heart breaking that I would return again to hear the soliloquies of these lonely fields,

Lamenting the absence of those radiant faces who once used to invade them,

To learn their summer lessons to break free.

4. It's October Again!

It's October again!

The acrylic dreams painted in the autumnal sky,

Resonate with the sweeping promenade of,

The freshly fallen lustrous golden leaves from the deciduous trees.

And once again in this souq of autumn,

The amaranthine fusion begins amongst magic, music, and dreams.

Now nature has changed sides to celebrate the colourful tides of autumnal fall.

It is as if the falling leaves have turned a new leaf in the cycle of change,

While performing their duty-bound seasonal role.

It's October again!

In Chateau de Autumn, the mead of life would be served without further ado,

As the festivities begin humming the mellifluous tunes of autumnal hymns.

A fragrance, luminescence remains ingrained in its milieu,

Giving a clarion call to everyone to unabashedly embrace its hues.

It's October again!

The kharif crops hitherto nestled in the soil would,

Now be harvested with much care.

And the sonorous tintinnabulations of,

Fulfilled hearts would be palpable everywhere.

It's October Again!

It seems that the waltz of autumn has an unfailing rhythm,

That is pulsating unanimously throughout the length and breadth of our mortal kingdom.

It is beyond doubt that the harvest, the falling leaves, the festivities all along have,

Collaborated to create these majestic, defining moments of autumnal song.

5. The Frosty Friend

Winter is known for its sombre tales,

Its colours are interpreted with harsh details.

The poets and artists portray its pain,

'Winter is coming!' is their joyless refrain.

Winter is harsh, winter is cold,

Winter is dark, winter is bold.

They say it designs a difficult game,

A masculine season with untamed flames.

It is often pitted against the feminine spring,

Which blossoms the earth like a wealthy queen.

Spring is profusely praised for its grants,

It is the winter which bears the brunt.

But there is lesson in winter's tale,

It teaches 'to strive, to seek to find and not to yield 'without fail.

Its harsh trials make us realise,

We must clear the hurdles before leading life
king size.

Winter brings out our inner strength,

It forges our determination to start again.

Its harsh doses have a valuable teaching,

That every cloud has a silver lining.

Hence winter must be deemed important,

It must be spared from our harsh judgement.

Its untrodden path must be welcomed without
reluctance-

For the cycle of life is understood best,

when winter is interpreted in its true context.

6. How Much was Too Much?
(Pentastich poem)

How much was too much?

The passing whistling wind inquired the heathen heath,

Which stood consumed by the pervading vastness of its existence.

The vast stretch of barren nothingness answered with reticence,

For this vastness and silence was all it had.

The wind now baffled, stupefied by the silence, asked itself,

Oh! How much was too much?

For the heath humongous, went beyond an onlooker's lens and

Defying the narrow perimeters of length and breath,

Outstretched its limits to touch the horizon.

The heath didn't take offense on the wind's interference,

For the inquirer seemed to be bewildered by its extension.

How much was too much?

To it, this query sounded as a sonorous refrain,

Reflecting the inquirer's deferential tone of reverence towards it.

It had carried this baton of extension for too long,

To be taken for granted and knew its worth went,

Beyond the temporal rise and fall of tides of time.

Really, how much was too much?

Only the capricious maker of the heath could answer it.

The wind finally got an inkling about the maker's whimsicality,

When it travelled afar and still found the heath there.

For nature had set no limit while designing her favoured masterpiece,

She had never paused to ponder,

How much was too much?

7. Lavender Smile

The heathen, unsullied lantanas,

Carefree beauties of the wild,

Graces the dormitories of,

Hills, plains, and valleys,

Wearing their lavender smile.

A chance glance at it,

Uplifts the spirit of a troubled soul,

One starts to believe in miracles,

While marvelling at their lavender robe.

The lantanas wear their lavender smile,

While facing hails, storms, and stress,

Sending us a powerful message,

That someday love would reappear to wipe away
all our tears,

That someday all our grievances will be
redressed.

The rejections, the failures,

The grievances, the silent tears,

All seems, in their presence, things of a distant
past.

And hope springs in the human heart,

By witnessing how they stand tall even at difficult times,

Still retaining their everlasting lavender smile.

Note: Lantana is a genus of about 150 species of perennial flowering plants of the verbena family, verbenaceae. Lantanas are seen almost everywhere in the north -east part of India, specifically at Guwahati in Assam, where I was born and raised. Though they can be found in different colours, the lavender- coloured lantana is my personal favourite.

8. An Ode to the Sunflower

In the deep quagmire of mirthless thoughts, of a truly lost soul,

Hope hops like a rainbow, appreciating your role.

You are resplendent in the radiance of sun,

Unmasking that perennial bliss of life, which will never wane.

You are aptly christened as the flower of sun,

O sunflower! You hold the key for a long run.

A minute spend in your graceful presence,

Rejuvenates and reiterates life's essence.

The maddening voice of anxiety fails to have an impact,

As your gracious entry severs its distasteful contact.

We cross the vast spiritual wasteland of our existence,

As you deftly ship us from there, crusading against resistance.

You chaperon and guide us back to real life,

In a way that we travellers can appreciate it, despite of its unending strife.

For your sun-soaked beauty reminds the hopeless soul,

That there is so much to explore, there is still so much to behold!

9. Homecoming

The fragrance of jasmine flowers,

Gliding with a soft breeze,

Ferries with itself the tales of its land,

To its native, traveling afar.

The freshly brewed breeze,

Brings him welcoming news,

Unlocking the bolted doors of,

His deep-buried memories ajar.

And he lets himself immerse in it,

Raising a toast to it,

For some priceless moments,

Reliving the past.

Those known alleys, that brook unbound,

Her stolen kisses, his love profound,

Flashes before his eyes, revealing their beauty
paramount.

He feels as if they were beckoning him and
saying,

"Its high time that you pay heed to our entreaties,
dear friend,

Its high time that you seek refuge in
homecoming."

10. The Magnanimous Mountain

As the viridescent mountain,

Stand below the rainbow embedded colossal sky azure,

The passing wind becomes a minstrel singing a mellifluous ballad,

To celebrate the chronicle of a heart so pure.

For the mountain has withstood the ravages of time,

And has remained unruffled by the challenges, occasional hiccups in variable phases,

It has hitherto managed to stand tall, including all,

Never grumbling about the storm and stresses.

It has always adorned the cloak of hospitality,

'All for one and one for all,' it has chimed.

And has been living by its principles so far,

While dealing matters trifle and matters sublime.

The unadulterated love oozing from its core,

Touch the lives of its resident birds, beasts, and flowers without fail.

Its assurance that their ministrations and grievances would be 'heard',

Cure the discordant notes and let peace prevail.

Its altruism makes a wonderful revelation,

That there exists great love amidst God's creations.

A heart that beats for all sans prejudice would,

Surely discover the fountain of love, peace, and freedom.

11. Ode to a Sparrow

I behold you from my casements ajar,

As you alight for a few precious moments at our ivy-laced balcony,

A tiny, fun-filled feathery creature whose 'tweets' often gets muffled,

Amidst our dusty smoke-filled town's cacophonies.

You rejoice in your own way,

Viewing the blooming presence of hibiscuses,

Rhododendrons, marigolds, lantanas at our balcony garden,

And by doing a solo 'waltz', you exhibit your love for them.

I tell you, your dancing moves are quite infectious,

As I unabashedly try it a bit in my leisure hours.

Your resplendent presence,

Add colour and flavour to my mornings.

And it transforms my balcony into a perfect stage
to perform morning rituals like,

Reading newspaper while sipping coffee and do
some constructive musings.

And while helping me to do so, you also become
my muse,

Who fuel my romantic escapades,

By veering the course of my thoughts towards
finding happiness in small things,

Which would sustain my energy throughout the
rest of the day.

You tweet here, you tweet there,

Flapping your wings,

Injecting romance in my otherwise mundane
existence,

By tweeting sweet nothings.

The mere sight of such a happy heart,

Lift my spirit to initiate a refreshing start.

12. Fireflies

The humongous black mass of darkness,

Engulfing earth post eventide,

Augment the fear already present in the heart of
the faint hearted.

The redeemer of such nights, the fireflies,

Engage in an exuberant luminous dance,

Flickering hope, dreams, and romance.

The fireflies fly and glow, glow, and fly,

Piercing the labyrinth of darkness,

Unruffled by the all-encompassing presence of,

The spine-chilling silence which defines such
nights.

It is for them that,

The predators camouflaged in this blanket of
darkness,

Remains uneasily on their guard,

In the fear of being discovered.

It is as if they dance to the tune of,

That rebellious music of life which exists even there,

Defying the realm of fear.

Their glowing hope,

Remains open to be explored by us,

So that we too can find,

That music in life which inspires ignited minds.

13. The Travelogue of a
Hyacinth Girl

Amidst the free-spirited mountains of the
highland,

Where the dancing dandelions allured the flying
flamingos,

I saw her first riding her little pony,

And undertaking a busy-idle journey

While holding a bunch of hyacinths in her
nimble fingers.

The hide and seek soft radiance of the dimly lit
sun,

Peek booed its rays in her comely face.

But she didn't fight this intrusion,

Rather welcomed this invasion,

Heightening its radiance with her smiling,
carefree embrace.

And her pony as if taking a hint,

From its mistress with the hyacinths,

Nodded with approval to walk a few more miles
with a steady pace.

But lo! The girl tightly held her pony's leash,

And remained transfixed in that moment,

Savoring the highland breeze.

She endeavored to live a lifetime in that moment,

And then, to express her gratitude for such an
overwhelming experience,

Sprinkled the hyacinths in the grassy pavement,

Before embarking again in her journey,

To explore the bold and beautiful highland
scenes.

F.

Lightweight Singles

1. Pain

She had endured much pain,

Pain, which broke her heart,

Heart, which once belonged to someone,

Someone, whom she had loved.

Loved him, as if she was possessed,

Possessed was she like an Oracle,

Oracle, who refused to foresee the pain of heartbreak,

Heartbreak, which caused her debacle.

2. Memories

Memories, a mystic recipe,

Tastes both sweet and sour

Some memories are to be cherished for life,

While others are best left to be blurred.

The busy-idle, loving-loathing facts of our lives,

Designs an intricate maze-running game-

Where we may be lost sometimes,

To be rediscovered in new ways again.

3. What You Want to be?

"So, girl, what you want to be?" Asked everyone good-naturedly.

As a five-year old, I strongly recommended the post of a traffic policeman.

At twelve, I vetoed it in favour of Superman.

At eighteen, I wanted to ditch my studies to become a renowned actress.

In my twenties, I strongly favoured marriage over job and,

In my thirties, I prayed for a child or two, to play the part of mother dearest.

In my forties, I yelled, "What???Leave me alone everyone.

I am trying to have some rest!"

4. Marriage

She took her marriage vows with a pure heart,

By giving the seven rounds around the holy fire.

The marriage collapsed, mocking her vows,

And the holy fire consumed her funeral pyre.

5. Graveyard

In the graveyard, the silence says it all,

That the bell has tolled.

Amen! Peace be upon the resting souls,

Who have left for their heavenly abode, leaving
all.

Their epitaphs would showcase their legacies of
accomplishments and pride,

Giving homage to their final transcendence to the
other side.

6. Bangles

The round multi-hued bangles, just like our
round earth,

Bears testimony of a woman's fascinating journey
since her birth.

And become instrumental in portraying her a
'round' character,

In her own story, by defining her a true fighter.

Her story remains ingrained in the bangles of her
hand,

A jingling tale of survival in this rocky patriarchal
land.

7. Souq

Post eventide, the potpourri of merchandises of
the shop seems,

Steeped in the exotic oriental incense percolating
from the souq.

Its Surma laden, fez cap adorned owner is
animatedly hovering,

Around his half-mesmerized customer like a
genie straight from,

The pages of Arabian Nights, finally declaring, "
Believe me madam,"

" I am selling it to you in my purchase price!"

8. Arrows

Two converging winning arrows had an identical tale,

Their owners were once aimless and officially derailed.

Then they stood up for themselves and aimed right,

Adding perseverance, persistence, and a spirit to fight.

And when this time their arrows took flight,

They went straight to hit the bull's eye.

9. Let Me Be....

Let me be, I screamed,

Let me walk my chosen path,

At my own terms.

Let me realize my dreams!

I promise I would not whine,

If I fade and not shine.

For if I fail, my consolation would be,

That those mistakes were mine!

Know this that I am a living, breathing being,

Entitled to do my own things.

So let me take this leap of faith,

To create my own perfect, imperfect somethings.

10. Strings

Unfeelingly, he pulled the strings of my heart.

Some screamed an agonized, discordant note,

Some got damaged beyond repair.

Others broke and lay scattered like martyred
soldiers,

In the bloodied soil of my broken heart.

11. Fire

O, the fire in my heart!

Never yield, never extinguish.

It is your presence that sets me apart,

From the herd, who are undistinguished.

12. Eyes

If eyes are a window to one's soul,

Then how do illusions play at what we behold?

The thing is, our eyes see what it wants to see,

Turning a blind eye to the harsh reality.